Adam's Ribs

For PJ + Ryan

Adam's Ribs

poems by Terry Adams

La Honda Forever!

Thanks For Being
Neighbors!

Off the Grid Press, Weld, Maine

TA56@coastside.net

Terry (EVA)

Grateful acknowledgment is made to the following publications in which the poems first appeared: "Pietà," "The Touching," *Poetry*; "Linotype," "In the Rodin Garden," *Ironwood*; "Point of View," "Writing Home," *Witness*; "Burying the Bird," *The Santa Clara Review*; "The Funeral," *College English*; "I Believe in All Things Visible and Invisible," *The Manhattan Poetry Review*; "Leaving," *Quarry West*; "Breath," "After the Laying On of Hands," *The Sun*; "Antique Lace" *The Best of Writers at Work*; "The Childless Man," *The Spoon River Poetry Review*; "Motocross," *Sow's Ear Poetry Review*; "Inoperable," *Bellowing Ark*. Many of these poems also appeared in *Fresh Hot Bread,* the journal of the Waverley Writers. "Pietà," was reprinted in *Poetry Flash*.

The author thanks Dick and Sarah Maxwell, Auriel Yost, and Jim Standish, *in memoriam*. Among the living, I thank my wife, Eva Knodt, the Motley Men's Group (especially Tom Devine, for direct editorial help), the Waverley Writers, and the La Honda poets..

Copy editing by Janet Clark of Loma Mar. Original mentoring and continued advice and support, James Reiss of Oxford, Ohio. Photograph of Author by Brook Tankle of La Honda. Cover painting and book design by Michael Alpert.

All inquiries and permissions requests should be directed to the publisher, Off The Grid Press, or to the author, at ta56@coastside.net.

Off the Grid Press
P.O. Box 84
Weld, Maine 04285
www.offthegridpress.net

ISBN 978-0-9778429-2-6 / 0-9778429-2-4

This book is dedicated to my wife, Eva

Contents

Part One

Pietà

The son sits on the bed's edge,
always the other is tucked in:
the mother who is going to die
that night refuses the son's
goodnight kiss, thinking the cause
communicable. Thirty years later
the son is there again, suddenly
seeing his daughter as too beautiful
and vulnerable at fourteen
to kiss or touch in this place.
The one not kissed thinks she is bad
or he is angry, feels for no reason
she is dying, or he is dying
and won't say.

Inoperable

My brother pointed to the hairline on his neck,
to the softened missile shape, like a failed third ear.
He said the bullet started out next to his lung,
then lodged behind his heart for years. On the road
his life moved like a car in heavy traffic,
by little graces and easings, with the waitresses
he loved in their motor homes, while the wind
rocked them, so it felt like they were traveling.
In the shade of an overpass, he would sit
on his bag, his thumb out, and look directly
into the eyes of the drivers, or he would take
the patience he wished he could find
in a woman, and look away. She shot him
just below his fifth rib. He said it felt like
a solid punch. He turned and walked out
and kept going for years with the bullet
traveling all over inside him.

Adam's Ribs

I miss how Adam's rib made me longer,
how it protected my heart from the heels of angels.
I want it back inside me, and I want a new rib

from each woman who began each of my lives,
and another for each woman with whom I was a first
trauma, or joy.

These new bones will stretch me and lay me down
into the first and sufficient body of the snake,
in whose form and motion I will regain the soft sheathing

that has been exiled in women. My shape
will overwhelm the design of male,
the thrust of myself become

an advancing caress, a salient of gentleness, like the tip
of a root growing with a hiss – the syllable
prefixed to all humanness.

Rather than an intrusion, all my ribs in unison
would be my legs, loving the ground,
and my soul would slip easy and warm within.

The toil of all my days will love me again.
I will turn left and right, and left again in one
motion, finding my way through and among

the rocks, carrying nothing away.
My children will crawl upon the earth
and nest on the earth; will increase themselves

out of their skins and give their old masks to the earth,
over and over while still alive.
We will swallow along our whole length

and be as pregnant with our meals as with our offspring –
we for whom there would be no more longing based
on shape or absence,

who could never make with hands a thing divided
or broken from life.

The Childless Man

I

He holds one hand with the other,
looking for a position that will feel unfamiliar
for a few seconds,
or he lets one hand relax while the other fiddles
with the fingers until they seem lifeless,
or he folds them on his chest
so nearly without volition he can
believe they are levitating.

II

Every time he thinks of fathering he remembers
the uncompleted flourishes of minor civilizations,
the dim, pointless battles
with memorized dates,
the villages that left no trace,
the oceans, ice, and forests traveled and forgotten.
Children have shriveled off of him
like burned skin – have passed
like plagues, or
like the great unnamed prosperities,
into an endless boil of fetishes.

III

His seed, his little mortifications, his half-replicas of
someone missing, the scrambled
characteristics, distillations of his flesh he withholds
and re-absorbs
like forgotten details of an important dinner –
an incessant rhythm of need, a pile-driver train
of anonymous houses on wheels –
framing the odd faces he shapes from nothing
into the accidental voodoos of sleep.

IV

There is a valve in the deep sump
at the dark bottom end
of the world,
in the most poisonous place, which
brings the surest and
longest death –
which must be turned, and this is where the childless
man does his service.
When he turns the valve, his body turns
to ashes on the wheel, and a huge
breeze blows
the new souls in through the opening
at the opposite end of the world.

After the Laying-On of Hands

for Jonathan

A slowly dying man will show you
his new, gentle attention,
a posed thoughtfulness, which will shape his mind
as he passes through death. But this temperament
is alien to you, and to him, and you must not
address it directly.
He has given away his extra flesh
to the charities of darkness.
He has no buffer against your need to comfort him,
his skull seems to be breaking toward you
through his face, but that too
is a false demeanor that you must not
address. You must approach him as you would
someone you have lied to,
or someone you have given too large a gift.
You will wait for him to lift his hands
in that vague gesture reserved for enraptured priests,
bidding you to come,
letting you feel in his wrongly shaped chest
his pulse squeezed and thinned by tumors,
his lungs clutched like a balloon
a child has fallen against.
What he calls spasms are labor pains.
What you think is his pallor is the broken water of his grave,
washing him slowly into the earth.
His sweat is the caul of the newborn, returning.
He will not transform to wax or plaster for you,
nor turn you away from his horror.

He is an embryo feeling the vague drama
of his mother's life through
a scrim of stretched flesh,
before the forces beyond itself deliver it out against any will.
I dream I would heal him by touching him,
because I contain an excess of the battles with many deaths.
I would rest my hand on his tumor,
make it glow hot and golden
in the shape of his diaphragm,
dissolve the cancer cells into
a little Eucharist of waste, an abortion
of the fore life, but he will not finish
as a living man. He is becoming heavy
with earth, sinking into the furniture of his house.
He is laying away his life into
the bodies of his friends the way
they lay their hope away in him.
He has stopped trying to remember things
because memory has taken him over,
occupying all the gaps, leaving no room
for change, like a comb, laying him flatter
and finer against the skull
of the earth. We try to say things
of a weight to match his weight,
but he answers out of his lightness;
he speaks for the dead, but with the words
of the simply tired or bored.
The moment of death will seem like some accident,
some crash inside him,
the components of his spirit abandoning our grasp,
his last second never quite accumulating its precision,
our hands never quite getting through.

In The Rodin Garden

This is where the dead go.
It happens;
a saw blade comes loose toward my face,
maybe, then half my head holds
numbness, and I look down with what is left
watching my hand reaching down
without my asking it, to steady me,
and everything in my body
is calmly laying me down and by then
I am dead, but also some sort of an agreement
has formed among the dying ropes
of my wrists, calves and back,
which insists me into that posture
which pulls the earth best
around me, not the dirt-earth,
but the true, deep,
ore earth. It is so simple and comfortable,
like falling onto a stage,
in some theater where I know all eyes follow me
because this is happening to me,
and I take on one of those shapes that I am
not given to choose until that moment,
though I can mimic each one now,
liking the musculature, the defined,
finished bulk, the resemblance to life.

Forgiveness

I just want to tell you a wish,
and what good is that?
Six puppies and the mother dog shot,
white skulls with holes the size of pencils.
I found them in a clearing in some bushes
beside an Interstate 80 off ramp,
skeletons lined up neatly
like bodybags in the news from a minor nation.
They could not have sat still for this.
Something in me stops each time I try
to tell this story, because the murderer is inside it.
These are murdered words.
This is a murdered wish.
But I need you to know I wished for
the impossible. I wished
something other than insanity or cruelty
did the killing, and my wish
is a crime against understanding.
I am not art, I am not
destiny, so help me the skeletons lay
behind a bush beside I 80 where I stopped to pee,
and I can't stop thinking
of all the possible excuses
for the killer, all the kinds of desperation
living out there with a gun
and no face.

Part Two

First Knowledge

The last time I was allowed to sleep beside my cousin
we were seven – at the end of times
when visits were long, and beds were few and small
and damp and full of sharp elbows, knees, and toys.
She said she had a new rule:
No sleeping until she cries.

"Tell me about a kitten left out in the cold,"
she said. She scooted closer, laid her cheek on my arm.
When I told her the kitten died, she was quiet for a minute,
then she said

"Let's be babies in prison and we are so cold we
have to get very close to keep from freezing."
Then she wrapped her whole self around me,
shivered, and said

"You should shiver too. Something is bothering you, isn't it?
Let's pretend you want to cry, but you can't tell why,
and you don't need to tell me, really,
but you put your head on me
so I can hold you until it is OK."

I did that, and soon she was asleep.

I lay awake feeling her breath in my hair,
trying to hold still, because never before was there a quiet
like that between us.

I was still trying to think of what to cry about
because it seemed like I should do that for her.
So I imagined we would be dead together,
in a heaven a little way above the moon.
I could cry for us then,
and sleep.

Antique Lace

My stepdaughter called me into the musty back
of the antique clothes shop;
she had a lace bodice clamped to her sides
with her elbows, like a split cocoon.
She asked me to button her.
At that moment I thought this was
the exact limit, the tips of my fingers
almost touching her, the bodice gathering
her breasts tighter with each white button
I worked into its white loop.
Then she turned with her face level with mine,
her beauty there in her eyes, and said
next time her boyfriend would do that.
A month later she took me to dinner, reached
for my hand, dug her nails into the backs
of my fingers and told me
it had happened, and it was wonderful.
She knew I could not move.
She squeezed harder and said it hurt like fire,
like needles, and when I knew what she wanted,
when I closed my eyes, bowed my head
and turned half away, she said
it hurt just like that.

Michael Harrington's Mother

On our knees in the linen closet,
in the smell of laundry,
with her flowered robe hooked
above us, he pulled it out of a shoebox,
with a finger to his lips.
In forty years the closest shape
I've seen is the tapered
patch on plywood, narrower
than a rubber coin purse squeezed-open,
wider than an eye. He lifted it out
with his finger tips,
unfolded the cotton pad,
swore me forever to keep secret
his mother's blood,
that creased, black-red oval –
like the print of a kiss.

The Natural Arc

A graph of the equation of dread
on the x axis,
versus necessity on the y –
ant trail along a door sill
won't go straight,
it bellies inward at all mysteries,
a post, or a corner,
like the drape of a spider web.
One straggler-ant
is always distracted with the job
of divination, or memory –
Did we miss anything over here?
Or here? The ant-stream goes
both directions always,
saying this time we are up to strawberries –
veer a little to the left,
wobble to the right, saying
let me feel what you remember,
and I will go the way
you came.

Part Three

Linotype

My copyboy guide walked me down the vibrating stairs,
and further down,
into the stomping shuffle-clatter of rolling presses
in the basement of the TIMES, where the words
of my father shook the earth, spewed sparks and oilrags,
in the inked hands of pressmen in railroad caps,
heaving at levers, shouting
with hand signals in the bedlam. Barrels of ink,
rolls of paper big enough to roll me right out;
the blurred belt of news careening, taut across rollers
like a demented, captive worm-bird;
the conveyor-stream, with every hundredth folded paper saluting.
This is where his words took on the strength of pounding metal,
the certainty of riveted bracing I-beams,
welded wheels, the grinding truth
abrading the paintless concrete floor.
His description of the world reeling, fork lifted out into the trucks
that huffed and lumbered off
into the dawn of Indianapolis alleys. The folded-out
photos of naked women wherever a wall was bare,
between pica charts riddled with ink-blood.
And looming above all of this in the heart of the pressroom,
the Linotype machine,
like a mountain of gasping typewriters and gut-shot jukeboxes,
whose inventor, they told me later, went insane;
and the operator dwarfed at his blazing keyboard
who turns half way toward me in his chair,
who bends way down to my ear

and screams through all of this, "spell me your name!"
So then I screamed myself out,
letter by breathless letter into this ear with the hair
bristling out, and way around back of the machine,
a minute later, from the unimaginable tumble of precision arms,
pinions, vats of oil, flapping of shelves, and noise and heated air,
my name comes to me,
my name comes right out to me
wet and warm and shining with fame,
backwards.

Dove

The fall from grace for my father began
when he answered one of my questions, revealing
he believed carburetors are solid, like condensers or rotors,
not hollow like alternators or light bulbs. By that time
I had learned from the mechanics in the family
that all equipment is either solid or hollow; and acts alone
through the power of shape or chemical disposition; or serves
as vessel for subcomponents of equal or greater interest; and
is subject accordingly either to further disassembly, or
replacement. But today I thought what a wonderful facility
for ignorance my father had, as I watched an overweight dove
lift off with frantic and presumably feeble thrashing,
heard its involuntary aspirations as its wing beats squeezed it
like a small, tormented bellows. I remembered that doves are
hollow, and even the bones within doves are hollow, and I saw
flight as vacancy in bones attacking the broader and
intensifying vacancy of the upper air. Where there is nothing,
there is a desire for greater nothing.

The Shortener of Stories

My father's eyebrows were heavy black lines
through my adjectives.
His frown proclaimed my finite clause insubordinate.

He would palm the carriage return and slam it back
while in the margin my voice would crack.
He wanted me triple spaced with no strike-overs,
and he filled the waste can
under the City Desk with my issues.

He let my monologue languish with the tape curling
under the teletype.
He crossed out whole pages.
I learned to keep to myself all predications

I was not prepared to lose.
He's the reason I never trust the news.

Cincinnati Ohio River Aubade

I could not have foretold while drunk and dreaming
in my eighteen-year-old body, this memory
of sleep, preserved in blackberry-vine and diesel
smells, in the water-flavored July air,
while the undertow of the Ohio sipped the edges
of the sandbar.

I dreamed I wanted to run with the river
down the cracks between the states, like silver,
while my friends kept casting their fishing lines all night.
I remember idly watching high overhead headlights
running up and down the suspension-bridge girders
like the hands of old people,
and car tires humming on the perforated steel bridge.

I remembered the little natural resource symbols,
shovels, smoke stacks, printed on high school wall maps
of Cincinnati. I wondered what should be the symbol
for the whorehouses in Covington across the river.
I imagined the moans of the whores
as they refused every morning to lease their bodies
to a cheap sunrise.

The river was digging the line deeper
between my states, sucking white junked
appliance bodies out of the creeks,
soaking garbage down into slime,
dissolving the soaked-off dander of bathers,

at once the boiling, gargantuan bed-road
for coal barges and rusty iron caskets of ore,
and the infinite tiny waters that parted
around my dangled hand.

I felt the river flowing with a rapture
projected from the dilated pupils of parked highschoolers
looking up now and then from the scenic overlooks
to relieve their suspended love.

And the river shimmered in reply to the stares
of the sleeplessly prayerful, and mumbled
with the snores of derelicts under the City docks,
and its dull sheen was the baldness of our fathers
reflected by moonlight on polished headboards
in suburban bedrooms.

And I became one of the dreams risen in the black mist
on the flowing stealth of waking water,
ebbing outward from among the reeds
hair-washing in the backwaters,
wafted and flavored with stink in the false starts
from the river's un-cemented banks.
I felt myself drawn out by the roots
onto the far shore of Kentucky,
where the thoroughbred souls were waking,
a while before their shining bodies wake,

bone and muscle of rolling water-light, moving under
the false shine of near-dawn, motion
already alive in the kinship of bluegrass and water,
horse dreams running unbridled through

the white-fenced pastures,
shuddering past the crossroad neon of closed bars,
flow of horse-souls flickering
against four-boarded white fences in the waning dark.

My dream told me to run like them,
before I am tied, before I am curried awake by groomsmen,
before the races begin for someone else's money.
And I knew that the horses were already up and running,
for themselves in the predawn, horses
without whose ungainly, rising grace the world will not tick
one arc-second further into a July morning,
with the twitches of the blue-tick hounds asleep at the
wheel of fox-control, in the feed-bins,
in their own half-sleep spasms of drunken freedom.

Lord, let me outrun this tired life where I am
tied by food, whose bonds ease at night on my ankles
like the wet rawhide the natives are said to
have tortured us with, and eased by the fiat of this
river with a lock lost in it, and floating doors, and one example
of each comfort contrived for this century
and disposed as junk.

The river aches and stumbles with the lost, and
the unburied remains, dark, wide, and low,
past the swarm of hay smells, the white-knuckled,
barge-pilot flow of dingy Midwestern prelight,
at the adolescent confluence of belief and rage,
its tributaries named into history by riots,
built by the tectonics of thugs seeking liberty,
and by the blood-blither of erosion,

semen dissolved and wafted from the discarded condoms
from good boys, mixing with the spent shower water
of Matriarchs.

Nothing floats all the way to the Gulf
alone, nothing un-mixes that is once mixed;
every illegitimacy is flaunted in the dream-water;
every tired marriage is forgiven in the long gospel
of grease and mud.

Oh I drank myself to sleep on the sandbar. . . .
I drank myself into a trick in the minds of my friends;
I gave the method of my awakening over
into their hands,
And they woke me in the dawn's early light
with a firecracker blast,
and in the red after-flash, I saw straight into the mouth
of a dead catfish they had lain on my chest.
I saw all the way into the pink and yellow gills,
as into some dilating death canal, into the scale-armored,
awful depth of our morning meal.
With my buddies howling, that one instant was on me,
through me, and gone; and I was awake,
shaking and cold beside the river.

Getting It Wrong

I can still hear myself gearing down
those twisty park roads, exhaust note echoing
off Brownstone townhouses on Hatch Street,
returning to that final and swankiest parental home.
Cranking my Harley up to 50 on the last straight block
of Celestial Street was my own long breath taken in,
lifting my naked eighteen year-old chest on those wings of sound.
I was reaching out to them, caressing them, reaching for their ears
and eyes, offering myself as the one free piston
filling the lungs of the race with glory,
pumping the soul of the city clean of its quietness,
in my suit of split air, on the job beyond the job.
I was the sum of my accelerations, to be heard in power,
to be the slithering white line a boot heel below my life,
my footpeg scraping sparks from the concrete,
tires painting a black lick of uncanny control, a storm self-brewed
between gravity and balance, streetlights flickering on my chrome
like lightning.

I felt in me the quiet fury it all ran on.
I was the world's own lover, tearing off everyplace in a graceful snit.
I could feel how I sounded and it was better than anything
that would get me fed or loved or taught.
I sensed the air flirting with me, tickling me with my own hair,
my engine thudding stronger than any footstep,
my knuckles chilled, my chaffed crotch eased with a brief
side-saddle twist. I believed they would surely sense
all this around me, the after-glow figurines dancing

out the back of my head, the photo negative
transcendence of the crack in the road
that could have killed me,
immortalized in mercury-vapor stagelight,
the hot blue chrome ticking at them in my eyes
in the washed-out air of our kitchen.

And then the exhale.
Braking for the last, mild turn between parked Cadillacs
on the doorman-haunted, footlighted driveway.
I was deflating myself
so I could squeeze back into my parents' home,
rolling slow on a perfect arc, triceps bulging, sitting upright,
all the neighbors watching me idle down into the parking garage.
One last tweak of the throttle made the concrete shiver
right under our apartment.
Then I bent down to flick the key off
and stopped right there,
to tell myself, that's not how they would ever
think of me at all.

Family Retainer

Whenever we talked she made it plain I was
someone other than my parents' child.
She was an angel of Jesus' blessed poor so good
I could hardly look at her,
so prior injured she was condemned to sweetness
toward anyone who was less than anybody else.
She looked to me like some kind of pie or a thing
abandoned on an altar.
I was a child a little past my prime.
We were given to each other as who would be
around the house when the owners were not – capitals
of hostile and repressed colonies – but we never talked.
They said she inquired of me from all her vacations to Florida,
and I was required to send her cards.
Precious few words ever written can say as much nothing.

We never talked.
We were different movies showing on the furniture of the house.
She was a Civil War of promises, gold braid, temperamental horses,
and mud. But I was James Dean playing chicken
and Sal Mineo's slide under the piano.
The harder I lounged, and left empty plates
on every surface in the house,
the harder she scrubbed, the wider she smiled, the deeper
she bent, and we never talked the most
when we were alone.

Dad moved out and she cleaned for him on Tuesday,
which was my day there too,
so I began to understand
how we each traveled with the furniture,
and she was the attending angel of furniture.
No one else had ever let me be
as silent.
When he died I brought her to the wake where she sat
guardian over what would not be said and
I understood, Lord, this underside,
this love around his ashes, a monstrous stone-polished feeling,
ancient black grandmother-stranger queen.
I brought her there so she would show them silence
for me, show them the grave
that had been following us all along.

Taking Over

In my dream I have been summoned
to give my stepmother away,
and I must contact the bishop to arrange
for cars, but I have been overseeing
a well-drilling by a team of three
small Irish workers who need to keep
reminding me that I already paid them.
They are bothering me while we sit
inappropriately soiled at the reception
where her new husband is a slime ball
sitting on my left, who doesn't know how
to talk, is fat with dyed hair, and
who believes I'm famous for something.

Point Of View

They came to me
in a dug-out listening post outside Da Nang,
handed me a green trombone with a rubber eye-piece.
They said Captain from now on
your name is Foxglove,
your social security number is secret.
I pointed the scope into the dark defile,
found three shapes burning amber
beyond the wire. Their hot armpits and crotches winked
as they stepped around the cool vegetation.
Rifles cast infrared
keep-out bars across them.
At ten meters I got them with the muffled
M-16 strapped under the scope.
It sounded like a stifled sneeze.
I looked out again,
one was moving, I fired again –
they were just little, quiet piles of light.
All night as I scanned I saw
the bodies cooling, becoming
smaller, dimmer, the hot head-crowns fading last.
This was the safest I'd felt in months. After dawn
I went out there
to tag them. There wasn't a sandal, no
bodies, not a goddamn
fingernail. In my hole
I lit my ration stove, cupped my hands for
warmth, and whispered my new name
into the flames that were disappearing in sunlight.

Writing Home

Later in base camp the soldier leans over his letter.
His dog tags let go of his chest,
swing into the air, and point down to the words.
His name,
rank, serial number, and blood type
swing out over the river where he saw the boatman hiding with a rifle
among his family, in front of the little outboard.
His dog tags swing over this letter that can say nothing
to a woman and child allied with a man at war about the enemy
who will shoot,
who wanted to swing over them on a vine
in a Saturday morning television-jungle,
on one of those magical arcs allowed by heaven
to the good, the strong, the faithful;
to take them suddenly and politely
away by the waists,
the small pith-helmeted woman and the folded-up child,
before the whole squad saw them.
The ratcheting spray of splinters, smoke and shattered water –
this letter with the river running over it
with the words of the river rising
as the squad scrambled down the bank,
to the surface of milky water,
and the satiny bubbles of soaked cloth,
suggesting arms, legs.

Part Four

Jazz

Jazz is a man starting over and over
on a problem he has leisure to solve,
watched by people who solved their own
too soon.

Jazz is the man snagging your eye,
wondering if there's anything he likes
in the purse in the lap of your lover.
Jazz is the man begging for your soul,

who paid his own in advance at the door.
Jazz is the man you looked at earlier,
who you catch looking at you now,
the white in his eyes singing intelligence

and poison. Jazz is the man who makes you think
your face has regained the chiseled beauty
you lost in the war with your television.
Jazz is the man playing to the fronts

of people's backs. He's always putting his hand
where there's never been a hand before.

Balls

This is the lower one, and this is the upper, she says.
Split level nuts, I reply,
townhouse nuts. She is examining me
closely and lovingly – places
I used to cringe at the thought
of anyone seeing, the places with covering
that doesn't quite qualify
as skin, with awful, soft wrinkles
veined like infant heads
barely haired over, that roll and flop,
resisting nothing – which sleep the day away
warming and sweating in the cradling hours,
like half-born Siamese twins, marsupialed
to the father, lolling
in idiocy – which seem to loosen,
crush, and wad a little more each year.
Then she runs her fingers all the way
back my underseam, over those legendary
folds that have enlarged also,
where one is never clean enough, one thinks –
places that tingle now at the brush
of her fingers, awakening to shy little alien
tickles, that have been submerged since
the final diapering a half century ago.
Now this midwife delivers away the ugliness
like some kind of ancient forebirth, welcoming
by her touch these living twins
who have come full term, healthy, red
and wrinkled.

The Dump

EACH each
            EACH each
say the gulls on the trash hill.
I've rumbled in here with a dump truck
in the lowest of twelve gears,
disgorged an entire
hundred-year-old kitchen with one lever.
I have read the dimensions a dead
carpenter wrote,
43 x 96,
his crayon still blue
on a splintered redwood stud.
I've come here with my wife and child,
raking the over growth of last year's garden
from a rented red trailer.
I've come with a dozen drifter-helpers
over the years,
yanking the remains of old bathrooms,
outdated kitchens, rotted porches,
out of a van.

I have come
in deep winter mud, and when
the trash is blooming
uncontrollably white and yellow
in Spring,
and I have come for myself,
and alone.

I threw our toilet eight feet
over a crushed electric
train set. It toppled
to its eternal reward, bottom up on a
box spring,
then I lofted the vanity sink,
with the hair of people I love still dark
and soaped, stringing
from the drain.

EACH each
            EACH each
My father's keys I've kept fifteen years,
to nothing.
His fourteen broken watches.
The knocked-down garage shelves.
A stuffed cotton-shark
with its jaw flapping.
The Apache have a word, *Alayah,* that means
"changes while flying through air."

Alayah, Alayah
the lead downspout inserts.
Alayah the pitted faucet escutcheons
that fit nothing else.
Alayah
what I saved to no earthly end,
leftover p-trap compression washers,
random nuts
for emergencies that did not come
in time,
cracked slab of white oak,

bent white cafe-curtain rods with three
jammed hooks, components of every whole
thing no longer whole,
carburetor rebuild kit leftovers,
amputated car radios,
infested red cushions, broken, painted bricks,
spare tire bracket, straps,
flattened, cheap luggage, holding airline ticket stubs
and pennies, and the smells
of perfume,
Alayah,
which I let fly into the untraceable
aura of benzine, skunk, paint,
rot, dissolving cardboard, and bleeding pens.
I go there two days in a row and the stuff
is already plowed under, the road
is plowed under.
The guard has moved his
bench and the portapotty.
Alayah
the dozer itself,
missing a tooth from its toothed wheels, and a blade the size
of a table for ten
shakes and tamps the hill.
Once I left an entire motorcycle
and watched the guy nudge it over almost lovingly with the dozer.
The spokes exploded like soda straws
while the wheels seemed to wobble upright again.
Alayah
It flipped along end for end up the mud hill
for a while, folding one way
and another; the frame wrapped itself

around the motor,
then it tucked itself
under.
Alayah.

The Flight

Just as I began reading over her shoulder, the young woman sitting ahead of me on the airplane turned to an intense sex scene in her novel. She was so absorbed I could see her pulse shaking in her hand. I noticed that her husband was reading also, out of the corner of his eye, holding a book in front of his face, trying as hard as I to make no anxious move that would get him discovered. When my daughter was a teenager I thought I had the privilege of witnessing through her eyes the female side of the battle to learn and be in control of sex. I was alternating between reading the passage in the woman's book and watching the sides of her eyes to detect where she was looking, so I could find the phrases she lingered over.

This woman whose name I'll never know was transfixed. Her hands were trembling. She was alone in that American Airlines seat with sexual images radiating through her body from the heat of her mind. She was so alone and protected there, in that place the words were imagining for her. It was like watching a general calmly assessing the slaughter of children, or seeing in the corner of the eye of a driver who has just hit and run, the glint of panic and finality, a passion to hide somewhere impossible to hide. Then a sudden glance passed from her, to her husband, to me, which contained the impossibility of acknowledging the state we were in, in which an aura of distain came over all of us. Then we sat back with an easiness that almost passed for ignorance, which was so powerful I can understand why the word sin was invented, and later forgotten.

Breath

They told me when I awoke to this body
        each breath will taste my blood
with the tongue of every creature that has lived,
        and I said yes.
And the air I breathe will be torn by rocks
        abraded by fans and bruised in the factories
of steel, and I said yes.
And they said the ants have a right to this breath
        as much as I, and it erases their paths
as they walk and as easily,
        it erases mine.
They said my breath will read me from inside
        with its licking torch as if I were a cave,
and I said yes.
And the air will carry the breathless
        patience of stone and the seething heat
of asphalt and scatter me from the memories
        as flickeringly as footsteps,
and I said yes.
The air will stir the wet of my body
        in the ocean of bodies, and in shared bodies
of hives and cities, and in the poisons,
        and I said yes,
I will breathe air that has passed through the nail holes
        punched by children into jar lids
to save the lives of fireflies, and I say yes.
        I will breathe the force that blows windrows
in snow, and rubs waves in the sand,

strips topsoil from farmlands
and makes the cypress cringe from the sea.
Though it is sour with dreams and loud
with sickness, it will run beside my heart
like a young girl beside a horse,
it will forgive my legs for running,
and chase my mind away from its fear,
and I say yes,
I will blow into whirlwinds in the breath
of my lover, and into sea storms I will fly to be healed,
and to the vastness inside clouds I will go
for rest, and I will wash out my tears
with the mist blown from white caps,
and disperse my venom in daggers of sunlight,
and I say yes,
I will torture my vision through
with the everlasting scanning of seabirds, yes,
I will breathe each layer from the horizon,
and hush my thoughts in the deepest calm of caves,
and ripple the slow, sunken rivers, like sleep,
then whistle through blow holes hidden in thickets
linking the underground to the sky.
I will whisper through the perforated coinage of sewer lids,
I will lie down in hot valleys with the breath
of vegetables, and I will say yes.
I will breathe a clear cloud of silk around my heart,
and wear a frayed scarf of fire.
I will breathe what determines the path
of falling feathers,
and blows snow from the seared summits
of mountains. I will stay trapped
a thousand years in a tomb until a mouse will free me.

I will whisper a cloud on the final mirror
of the dying, before the cistern of silence cracks,
and I will make a quick slate
for fingers shouting behind cold glass,
saying yes.

Part Five

The Touching

I did not pull away in time
for this to be a bump
and he did not react quickly enough
so we are stuck with my knee touching the tip
of his elbow.
I can't think about anything else
and I can't seem afraid or aware and he
must not pull away as if
he wanted to pull away
because I would wonder why.
I listen for the weather of the room, the rhythm
in the floor, the color in the iris
of the middle distance
to provide a distraction, so I can leave
with no reason,
as with no reason I came together
with my brother and
for fear stayed attached
until freed.

The Passage

What has passed easily between them
in twos as deepest care
now whirls like a small wind
among these three,
saying good-by in the former lover's
entryway. He helps them on
with coats, while nodding that he
is now her past, where there is no
anger. The new lover mentions the death
of a friend, so they all feel
grief for a moment as a heaviness
in their skins that have slept against
each other, and touched politely.
The woman who moved between the men,
and changed them both,
says she will bring her mother
to visit the old family a few days before
Christmas. And the old lover turns
to her asking for the health
of the mother, and then it is time
to take her back in a hug,
so she slides against him almost the way
she did back then, before she steps back,
making way for the hands of the men
to come together, which will involve
the brief laying-on of the unclasped left hand
of each, and the final motion
begins in the new lover's arm

as he touches her shoulder,
using the new signals, which
surround them like smoke,
and the small dog of love whose true
master seems unknowable
precedes them all into the night air.

Miscarriage

It will always signal a weak spot
on the earth for them,
the memory of the strength they spent
so easily, walking naked up slabs
of granite beneath scrub pines,
high and deep in the mountains, when
the first child in either of
their lives melted, gave up,
or was pulled as the doctor guessed
by the thin air, becoming blood,
becoming the future running simply
away, bright and beautiful, with
no physical pain, a rivulet
on a sloped rock beside the Stanislaus,
where the river is four feet wide
and a quarter-inch deep every
July, and the seven-week pregnancy
they had named Spring let go,
and they watched her run
beside the river and join the river,
becoming a red wing.

The Seizures

When it was over I sat her up in bed and began to untangle
the mats in her hair.
I stretched the masses sideways until I could see through them,
and I picked the edges of a knot
until a few strands came free. Then I held tight near the roots
and brushed hard until she started to cry,
then I worked the larger mats again, with only my fingers.
I would give up one place, go to another,
and when I began to think of the idea of fault,
or how I had no idea how one is supposed to do this,
I would need to find another place to work on,
but then I got lost in smaller tangles I didn't recognize, and she was
leaning toward the side I was combing
as if she was unconscious,
so I turned her to the light and brushed the hair
that was free, smoothing with my other hand along behind the brush,
until I could find enough to make a soft,
black wing, and lay it over her shoulder. Then she
reached up and rested her fingers lightly on my fingers, on her hair, and we
sat still a while, until we both believed
she would stay in this world a while longer.

X-Ray

Before they would let us see the x-rays
I didn't know what else to do
but feel your head,
for the place that could be
too warm or cool, or soft.
Your hand followed
on top of my hand
over your brow and eye-sockets,
the shape of your skull
coming alive in the subconscious
of the body. You began making a sound,
like a voice calling the name
of an animal into the night,
and when I listened as hard as I could
I heard you ask: why is it
so hungry?

The Funeral

It starts in the feet
of men walking with a casket
down stone steps.
As it rises their faces slip away
leaving only the faces of the crowd
mirrored in shiny cars
moving cautiously, wearing scarves
and veils, out past the iron gates
where it reaches the loins
and begins to stir the leaves in the grass
about the feet
of men walking with a casket.
They arrange themselves around
a hole, open
into the face of the afternoon
and the emptiness moves
up to the stomach from the grass
trembling gently.
From there it rises anxiously
at the bidding of holy hands
over an open book,
open to the faces of others.
The casket is lowered
and it follows downward
draining off the fingertips
of benediction, pouring
from all around, from the fingers
into the grave

beyond the velvet ropes
where the silence joins
the silence of the dirt
and the whispers of those
left above.

I Believe in All Things Visible and Invisible

My aunt stirred the trash fire
making black nests of ashes unroll.
It was our job to watch it burn;
to keep it from blowing away.
Chicken bones cracked,
cigarette packages puckered,
the foil shimmered and waved before it disappeared.
I saved my mother's empty pill bottles and filled them
– some with pepper, iodine, milk,
pine needles and Ivory Soap –
and I tossed them in there with the shriveling
cereal boxes, the cans with flames swirling inside.
Some I filled with my bath water, my spit,
a spoon of beer and talcum,
the ash of a Lucky, a hair from the sink,
coal dust from the bin, and cologne;
my fingernails, the holy water
I had stolen, some candle tears, a button,
a stone, a gold star from catechism,
match-heads, and a penny.
I froze the pill bottles in the snow by the backdoor
and put one in every fire
the winter I was nine.
And once I saw Flash Gordon unroll from the flames,
his face glossy with melting bacon fat
                    – he burst into gas
before I could read what he was screaming.

Leaving

Mother had me up with all the lights
before dawn;
her head seemed to turn a certain new direction
no matter where she looked.
I imagined the way to be all downhill because anywhere
on our globe was down from everywhere else.
I can't feel him, I said.
She said come here, brought me out to the curb and had me
step one foot down onto the street.
She waited. I said nothing. Cement, she said,
once you are on cement you can get anywhere,
at least in America. You can get to anybody,
even your father, in America, through cement.
I've grown up with a feeling we are all traveling across
pack ice. Light is everywhere. Many families are filling
the little river valley that points the way.
Groups move off at intervals
then send back for forgotten things,
or they actually visit backward, and those of us who
have not left go out along the trail
to spend one night or two with friends. The children
are the busiest, coming back two or three times before
they are out of sight.
Always along is an adult still young enough
to be honored with mild censure by parents,
who excites the children with wild stories
and gestures of what to expect.
Just after dark the calm and hugely competent

middle people gather. Their talk continues,
soothing into the sleep of the others.
It was our tradition once the waving began
to keep it up until the other was completely out of sight,
so the first steps of all our travels were made
backward, until the second or third stumble
by the one departing, who would turn away
for several steps, and always suddenly look back to see
the hands of those standing and watching rise again, and their faces
opening with a little laugh as if they had been tagged
in a game.

Motocross

Suppose I do a little jump to start,
slightly sideways like a standup comic,
or pull my front wheel up and brandish my
handlebars like a flat offering of gold
as I fly past the green flag you are holding?
Then spin around and widen my eyes at you
as if I am listening, even though it is me
who is talking like crazy.
Right away I learned to slide the
rear wheel out, like risking a touch
on a young girl's waist, pressing myself
into shape of the turn, until a certain
lightness collects in my spine and I chop
the throttle, which might high-side me into
the weeds, or slide me down gently in the dust
if I am lucky. Pretty soon I get it that I must
commit to the turn, to the faithlessness
of the turn, prepare my body into a guess
where the grooves in the track cross.
Suppose she is not the one I love?
Smoother lines? New lips every time?
I learned to scoot up over the front wheel
to sense the pressure a swath of ground will hold,
make the wheel bite and rail me in an arc. I tell her
everything about myself the first day after
the first sex, so the misunderstandings that are
fresh don't repeat immediately, and she says
yes again, the bike diving perfectly, setting up for

the next corner, bouncing to the edge of the track.
The pros will show you exactly how,
over the roar of your motor – Catch me! –
they yell, and one day I am
rattling handlebars with Bob Hannah on my home track.
I get him on the inside with a slick little pivot,
slam three times my weight into the berm. I am
the fastest rider in the world for two minutes,
and the next lap the same track is a different track.
This is where it happens. Can I see that the apex
has shifted like a polite waiter moving out
of the light? Can I see how fast the turn approaches
from how fast I feel? Can I stay interested
in her children and her earrings, the way
I scrub off speed, pitching the bike sideways
in the flat corners, time after time?
Can I remember what my life depends on
over and over? Do I know when
to drift away in the little art shop in the country,
and converge again quietly, with just one finger
on the outside of her wrist? Can I bear
the false starts, the sleep-twitches I feel when
the race is over, and she is still?

Part Six

Burying the Bird

The three of us simply found it dead:
no marks, no reason. We were nine.
Its head was loose
as a string.
We tried making our heads that loose –
tried lifting each other up
from as dead as we could make ourselves.
The wings pulled open and sprang back
like a soaked book.
We buried it with some prayers
beside the abandoned sandbox. Next morning we dug it up.
It hadn't changed;
we brushed it off, opened its wings – tried running
with it stretched by the wings between two of us
while the third ran behind holding the tail feathers open
like a kite.
We buried it again in the same hole
and showed some other kids where.
Next day they didn't believe us, so we dug it up.
One wing was stuck open,
the feathers at the neck fanned-back separately
like shoe brush quills.
We reburied it with a little procession.
We wrote "BIRD" on a magnolia leaf and
stood it up for a tombstone.
On Monday the leaf was gone, the head was stiff,
it was flat on one side.
This time we buried it with a baseball card.

Next week it looked like it was in four pieces;
no one would pick it up; Patsy cried.
We never went back.

Indian Winter

Erika picks up her pet rats
and flings them softly
out onto the lawn. They run back over under
and around each other,
so she scatters them again
out into the grass.
They follow her.
They climb her sox and her jeans.
She falls down all around them
into a corral of arms,
a mountain range of shoulders and elbows.
Her palm is a ferrying bird,
scooping them up with their tails whirling
for balance. She is a cavern-maze
of loose sweater sleeves,
a forest of fingers.
We have been waiting all winter for rain
and the clouds are showing signs of darkening above us,
so now she makes herself into a thunderhead
swaying from her knees, her hands
splayed in a double salute,
and she blows her breath around the rats, and widens her eyes
to be their lightning and rain –
                    to bring the lightening and rain.

Last Draft

I wrote a long poem on a kitchen counter made of wood planks in an abandoned cabin in the Southern California high desert. I took all afternoon. I broke my pencils – clogged the ballpoints. The words got smaller as the poem expanded. The sun shines through the roof and the planks are dry and cracking. Sand blows in. Mice shit on the words; pieces of the roof fall in. The cabinets beneath the counter are rotting. There are bullet holes everywhere. The walls are patched with sheetmetal. An old stovepipe rots in a corner, the single bed is rusted springs. The temperature reaches 125 degrees. There are hailstorms, sand storms. Somebody might pry the boards up and stick them under a truck wheel stuck in the sand outside. Maybe a lonesome drunk will vomit on it, maybe light a fire on it, stand on it trying to hang himself. Somebody will make love on it, or climb on it to get away from a snake. I was trying to evoke the free soul of the place – desecration, and sacrament – what it is like to love someone whose love is a damaged thing.

I was trying to write about whoever built the place, and everyone who has taken something or broken something in there. The cabin might be 20 years, or 90 years old. It is leaning and it will collapse soon – it is surrounded by black mining equipment, cracked retorts, shattered barrels, twisted wire fences. An old truck body. Piles of mine tailings.

This is in a canyon off Highway 168 on what is sometimes called Death Valley Road, sometimes Waucoba Saline Rd. If you go there, and you can read what I said, please contact me. Most of what I write is laying around someplace on a piece of paper. Sometimes I have this feeling I do not want to be left alone with what I write – or I want to forget it – I did not want to forget what I wrote there, but I did. I kept at it all day. It might be 1000 words. My feet got tired. My hand cramped. I didn't edit anything, and I felt driven, and free. I felt heard. Please find me. Call me.

I Want To See

I want to see everything written down
    I ever thought.
I want to read each delicate fern-end fossil of logic
    that gave its life at the frontier to nevermind.
All the nonsensical categories and counter-categories,
    calligraphy of flavors, the italic memories of odors.
I want worded the echoing caves where I first understood,
    and each sensation of singular time expanded to a phrase.
I want to see the concrete river half empty of my grief
    engineered through my city of derelict pronouns,
    the weedy patches of resolve pushing through the cracks,
and a throng of sunsets monk-robed in the lost pink ends
    to my twenty thousand days.
I want to see the names in light of everyone I've loved,
    in lesser light the ones I've loved a little,
    and for each time I've whispered a name
    I want it written in air,
and the thrill scrawled-out when my name was spoken
    or whispered or giggled or screamed.
I want to read the cipher of footprints in the meadow of my bliss
    and the wired-in savior ranting of my soul to itself,
I want caveats of my iron will welded in cursive on the
    iron casket of what I've refused,
the history of my arm-wavings fictionalized in my too-thick
    novel of goodbyes.
I want to see written every hopeful command to my fingers
    as I leafed through the labels of trousers at sales.
I want to see the breath of fresh sheets immortalized

under the heading of artificial winds.
I want my repetitions penciled-over like the initials of lovers
on park benches, and solid block printing
where I memorized poems.
I want to read again the groove in the lawn where my father
dragged our ashcan to the gate.
I want to see my fear burning horror movies
into bands of expanding celluloid holes.
I want names for the idiot drivers I have blowtorched,
a stamped leather concordance to my tract of lies.
I want to smell the detritus I have torched
from the skin of sentences.
I want to hear the growling claims of the under-persons
in my card catalog of anxieties.
I want bigger than life the proto-thoughts from
my infant brain, petroglyph stick figures
for confusion, the ruined stone tablets of clairvoyance.
I want to read the hand-smeared excrement on the walls of
my imagined confinement, fingerprints
on the flesh of my meditations.
I want to read what I said to myself while waiting for
the time to speak.
I want to see billboards of all the true things I've refused
to say aloud.

The child of newspaper editors, with roots in Cincinnati, Ohio, Terry Adams grew up in newsrooms and Catholic grammar schools. He earned an M.A. in Creative Writing and Literature at Miami University, Ohio. During the Vietnam War era, he became Top Secret Control Officer at the U.S. Air Force's Strategic Air Command Headquarters, where he had the opportunity to contemplate his personal role in the destruction of civilization. He left the service as a Conscientious Objector in 1972.

For many years he has been active in the local poetry community, including the Waverley Writers of Palo Alto, the Not Yet Dead Poet's Society of Redwood City, and the La Honda writers' group.

His poems have appeared in *Poetry, Ironwood, The Sun, Witness, College English, Bellowing Ark* and other journals. He lives with his wife in La Honda, California, among the giant Redwoods where he restored Ken Kesey's famous 1960s house. When not writing, he manages Public Works for the Community of La Honda.